Ponies
on Dart...

Felicity Young

Bossiney Books • Launceston

First published 1998 by Bossiney Books, Langore, Launceston, Cornwall

ISBN 1-899383-13-1

© 1998 Felicity Young

The photographs are reproduced by kind permission of Only Horses Picture Agency except those on pages 3 and 30 (Roy Westlake) and page 8 (Paul White)

Printed in Great Britain by Cornwall Lithographic Printers Ltd, Redruth

Dartmoor

There are many reasons for visiting Dartmoor. It is a wonderful place for walking, horse riding or just driving through in a car and admiring the beautiful landscapes. The scenery is breathtaking: stark open moorland and huge granite tors contrast with picture postcard villages nestling in wooded valleys.

Throughout this glorious countryside, and one of Dartmoor's favourite attractions, are the wild ponies. They live on the moor all the year round, sometimes enduring extremely harsh conditions.

At almost any time of the year the ponies can be seen in their herds. In spring they graze among the bracken and heather which provide welcome cover for very young foals left to rest by their mothers after a feed.

In winter they stand huddled together sheltering from the wind and rain, their thick coats matted with mud. The snow settles on their backs, but their winter coats are so dense and waterproof that it does not penetrate. They are pretty well equipped to survive the severe Dartmoor weather.

Native breeds

The British Isles have nine native breeds of pony: Fell, Dales, Welsh Mountain, Highland, Shetland, Connemara, New Forest, Exmoor and Dartmoor. Each of these mountain and moorland breeds has evolved in a particular way to survive in different conditions in different parts of the country. The Exmoor and Dartmoor ponies that are seen in the wild in the South West seem similar in many ways, but actually have their own distinct characteristics.

One of the first mentions of the Dartmoor pony appears to have been in 1012 in the will of a Saxon Bishop, Aelfwald of Crediton in Devon, where he talks about 'the wild horses on the land at Ashburton'. But little is really know about their origin. Ponies have certainly lived on Dartmoor for centuries and some experts say they have been influenced by much older Devon and Cornwall breeds that are now extinct.

Unlike the Exmoor pony which is believed to be descended from the native British wild horse and has changed very little, the Dartmoor may have evolved from the same original native type but then been 'improved'. The Romans may have brought over Arab and possibly Spanish stock, while a later infusion of Fell and even Welsh blood may have been used to produce a better, stronger and more beautiful pony. Many would say there are no 'pure' native breeds in Britain, because all at some time have been influenced by people and events throughout history.

In the past the very nature of the Dartmoor pony - sturdy, sure-footed, hardy and good tempered – made it an ideal working animal. In the nineteenth century they were always called 'colts' by the hill farmers, and were used around the farm up to the 1930s. They were even ridden by Dartmoor prison warders until the 1970s to escort prisoners to and from their work on the moor.

The Dartmoor pony's versatility and stamina also meant it was often bred with other types of pony to produce offspring that could be used for very specialised jobs. For example, during the Industrial Revolution Dartmoor ponies were bred with Shetlands so that the coal mines could have small but hardy pit ponies. And at the other end of the scale, in 1917 the Prince of Wales set up the Duchy Stud and bought Dartmoors to begin a breeding programme for an all-round riding horse.

Dartmoor Pony: the official breed

With the introduction of polo from India in the late nineteenth century, there was an increasing market for ponies with a bit more size but with the typical Dartmoor traits of nimbleness, quick thinking and plenty of stamina. Thoroughbred and Arabian stallions were successfully bred with Dartmoors to produce suitable stock. The Polo Society, later to become the National Pony Society, was set up in 1893, and six years later the Mountain and Moorland sections were opened in the Polo Pony Stud Book. This meant that a standard came into being for the Dartmoor pony breed and, apart from a reduction in height (from 14 hands to 12.2 hands), this standard has not changed.

In 1924 the Dartmoor Pony Society was formed and with this came official recognition of the breed. It has since gone from strength to strength, and today ponies are exported to Europe, the USA and Australia. Their wonderful temperaments make them ideal for young children, and they are frequently seen winning at ridden and in-hand shows, at Pony Club rallies or being driven in harness.

The wild ponies on Dartmoor

The Dartmoor ponies seen with their rosettes at shows are now somewhat different from their namesakes living wild on the moor. The 'Dartmoor Pony' is a distant relative of the 'ponies on Dartmoor', and it would be unfair to compare them. On the moors today there are far more ponies of mixed breeding than in the past, which has given rise to an increasing number of coloureds (piebald and skewbald). These do not match the 'standard' of the original Dartmoor, which is bay, brown, black, grey, chestnut or roan.

The introduction of 'mongrels' may originally have been an attempt to create pretty children's ponies, which sell better with white markings, but in effect it did the ponies no favours. The success of the Dartmoor as a native breed in the show ring rose while the number of ponies on the moor declined. The reason for this decline may have been that there are no government subsidies for raising ponies and, now they are no longer used on farms, there is little incentive for farmers to keep them. Breeding programmes tended to lapse, as strong stock for working was not a priority, and the ponies were left to roam and breed unchecked.

Such haphazard breeding over the years diluted the stock and many ponies no longer had the Dartmoor hardiness to cope with the harsh conditions: food was often scarce and so the ponies suffered. In the late 1980s it became clear that the survival of the wild ponies was in jeopardy.

Improving the ponies on the moor

To improve the standard of the ponies on the moor, the Dartmoor Pony Moorland Scheme was introduced in 1988. A collaboration between The Dartmoor National Park Authority, the Dartmoor Pony Society and the Duchy of Cornwall produced a scheme that would encourage the moorland farmers to return to breeding 'pure' Dartmoor ponies.

A registered stallion was turned out with a group of about fifteen approved mares and kept in a fenced area of the moor known as a 'newtake'. In the autumn they were gathered and returned to their owners to graze on the moor and to foal in the spring. This was very successful, and after the Dartmoor Pony Support Scheme was introduced in October of the same year the number of 'newtakes' was increased to three. These are still in use today.

The schemes have helped to halt the decline in numbers of ponies on the moor and have improved the quality of the stock. The next generation will all, hopefully, be strong and hardy and capable of surviving the cold winters.

If you are interested in seeing the ponies in their summer location, the Dartmoor National Park Authority organises special walks through the newtakes. The sites are right in the heart of Dartmoor between Two Bridges and Dartmeet. Access is allowed only on these guided walks so that the ponies' environment is not too disturbed.

In September the Dartmoor Pony Society holds a Moorland Show at Princetown on Carnival Day. This is a good opportunity to see some of the mares which have taken part in the scheme and to admire the qualities of the Dartmoor pony in the show ring.

The future of the ponies on Dartmoor

The pure Dartmoor pony is still in danger of dwindling, but The Breed Society, the National Park Authority, the Duchy of Cornwall and the Dartmoor Commoners have all played vital roles in trying to preserve one of Britain's best known and loved native ponies.

The Rare Breeds Survival Trust has also now stepped in: believing the Dartmoor Pony to be a vulnerable species, it has given it Rare Breed status. There will always be ponies of some description on Dartmoor, but it would be sad if the pony whose ancestors roamed the hills and valleys from before Roman times was to disappear.

Life on Dartmoor

Once the grass begins to grow in early April, the first crop of foals are born on the moor.

It is a good time to visit Dartmoor, when the bracken is sprouting green shoots and the heather is showing signs of life after a harsh winter.

The foals are born with a thick coat which gives them a rather cute, cuddly appearance.But its main function is to protect them from the spring weather which can be bitterly cold.

Nature makes it necessary for the new-born foal to stand as soon as possible in order to travel with the herd. It will make its first attempt to stand usually within half an hour of its birth, and will be up and sucking from its mother within an hour and a half: such is the instinct to survive.

The expression on a foal's face always seems to be one of surprise: foals are naturally very inquisitive and get up to mischief at an early age.

It can be fascinating to watch them from a distance, feeding from the mare, sleeping in the bracken or kicking up their heels in the warm sunshine.

You will see piebald and skewbald ponies on the moor, but these are not accepted for breeding in the newtakes

The mare is in foal for about 340 days and after foaling becomes pregnant again almost immediately if a stallion is running with the herd.

This explains why the mares, after producing a foal year after year, begin to look poor with sway backs and large bellies. In the wild this is a natural course of events.

The brood mares in the newtakes are all approved by the Breed Society and, though they may not appear to be beauties themselves, it is hoped will produce good foals for future stock. It's worth taking one of the guided walks to see the ponies and compare them with those of mixed breeding out on other parts of the moor.

As the foals grow through the summer months, they shed their shaggy first coat, looking moth-eaten for a while until they emerge in their somewhat sleeker attire. The short fluffy tail and tufty mane still remain to show that these youngsters are only recent additions to the herd.

Today there are few threats to the foals' survival in the way of predators, but a major threat to their safety now comes when they stray onto the roads and become victims of traffic accidents.

Ponies are often attracted to the roadside by well-meaning people who throw them titbits from their car windows. They then tend to congregate on the verges, looking for picnic leftovers, and are frequently hit by passing vehicles, especially at night.

Speed limits and a traffic control scheme have been imposed to slow down the cars and so reduce the number of casualties. Don't encourage the ponies by feeding them, but allow them to remain totally independent of humans.

Pony behaviour

Two distinct features of the Dartmoor pony are its full flowing mane and tail. A thick mane is a great asset in wind and rain, and a long forelock helps to keep the summer flies away from the eyes. The long tail is also a good weapon against the flies: the ponies can often be seen standing in a huddle, nose to tail, swishing away insects from each others' faces.

Watching the ponies in the wild shows how great the herd instinct is. We have domesticated the horse and separated it from its natural environment. We expect it to work alone carrying the weight of a rider, when in the wild anything on its back would be the utmost threat to its life and its natural reaction would be to buck, kick and flee. Ponies are gregarious animals: seeing them grooming each other and the special bond between the mares and their foals confirms this.

All is not harmonious, though, when two stallions meet and fight for supremacy over the mares.

A precocious colt may try to infiltrate the herd, but is usually put in his place by the stallion. Teeth are bared and hooves fly amongst a blur of manes and tails as they clash.

The youngsters learn this behaviour by play acting with their peer group, playfully nipping and rearing up to 'box' with their front legs. It is all practice for when they are old enough to challenge a rival for leadership of the herd.

The stallion, however, is not in charge on a day to day basis. There is usually an older mare who acts as a matriarch. Her role as leader includes being responsible for discipline within the herd and controlling unruly youngsters who get a little too cheeky. She is always on the look out and will alert her companions at the first sign of danger. In return she has priority at watering places and the best grazing.

Within the rest of the herd there is a strict pecking order. If you watch them you will often see continuous nipping and aggressive posturing by the ponies as they try to establish their position in the group.

At other times ponies can be spotted in small groups picking at the grass at the base of the lumps of granite strewn about the landscape. Grazing contentedly, their coats gleam in the sun and life seems easy and relaxed.

When autumn comes the ponies are rounded up in what is known as the annual 'drift'. Their owners are keen to check their stock, brand some of the ponies, sell the weanlings and turn the rest back to the wild to grow on. In the past the local fairs were popular places for the farmers to sell their ponies and to socialise at the same time.

The famous Widecombe Fair is held every year at the beginning of September and, although it has become more of a tourist attraction and less of a farmer's day out, it still has a wonderful atmosphere.

The drift

Many of the moorland ponies are destined to be sold, but before they can reach the sales they have to be rounded up and claimed by their owners. The drift begins with the farmers and their helpers gathering at a prearranged starting point. Suitably mounted on a variety of horses and ponies, they then disperse and round up the ponies from all four corners of the moor. This can mean riding for miles over rough ground and at quite a fast pace. At the end of the day the riders and their mounts are weary, but their task is accomplished: the ponies on Dartmoor are accounted for and contained in a holding area.

Above: ponies in the holding area

Below: a newly branded pony

Opposite: resting after a hard day rounding up the herds

Farmers sorting out their own stock from the rest of the herd

Opposite: ponies being driven from the holding area to the farm

Once in the holding area, the farmers can identify their stock and take them to their own farms where the foals are either branded and kept another year or sent to the local horse sales.

Years ago when ponies were plentiful the annual drift was a big affair likened to the huge cattle drives in America. There was a great movement of stock and it was a serious source of income for the farmers who got a good return for little or no outlay.

With hundreds of ponies gathered together in the holding areas, it must have been a huge spectacle.

The drift is still an important day and there is still money to be made, but numbers are smaller than they used to be and some of the ponies are of poor quality. It is sad to think that many of these animals may be sold for meat.

The sales

At the sales the welfare of the ponies is closely monitored. The RSPCA inspectors keep a watchful eye over proceedings. It can be a very stressful time for the wild ponies which have little or no contact with humans during most of the year and which suddenly find themselves herded off the moor and pushed from pillar to post.

For the very young it is especially traumatic, as they are often separated from their mothers for the first time. There is a great deal of noise: the clanging of the metal gates, people shouting, the voice of the auctioneer and the general hurly burly of the market scene can all be most distressing.

The presence of the RSPCA is intended to ensure humane treatment of the ponies.

It is not very dignified for them to be crammed into a pen with many others and to have a lump of glue and a label slapped onto their hindquarters.

In spite of all this there will be some lucky ones that will be sold to private buyers for children to cherish or else for use in riding stables. At the end of the day, they are loaded into lorries and taken to their new homes.

Winter

As winter approaches, the ponies grow their thick warm coats which will help to protect them from the driving rain and the icy winds that blow across the moor. They tend to gather lower down by the roads, finding shelter under trees and hedges which grow there. They look resigned to the fact that for the next few months life will be hard.

More time is spent standing close together for warmth and less time is spent grazing. The thick long tail that kept away the flies now serves to keep the wind and rain off the hind quarters, and the profuse mane channels water away from the neck and face.

The sight of these ponies, whether in winter or summer, cannot have changed much over the centuries. Roads now connect the more remote places of Dartmoor with the outside world, and the farmers have tractors and four-wheel drive vehicles to give them easier access to the land, but the scenery has not altered.

There are still vast open spaces of untouched moor, with massive granite tors rising from the bare landscape and grazing ponies still picking their way through the rough moorland grasses.

Pony trekking

An excellent way to see Dartmoor is from the back of a horse. There can be nothing better than riding on the moors on a clear sunny day in some of the finest scenery in Britain.

Pony trekking is one of those 'getting back to nature' pastimes which makes people who have never been on a horse in their life throw caution to the wind and venture out into the countryside.

Other more experienced riders may want to gallop wildly across open moorland with the wind in their face.

There are riding establishments to cater for all tastes. The British Horse Society (BHS) and The Association of British Riding Schools (ABRS) are two organisations responsible for maintaining high standards among riding centres.

It is advisable when looking for somewhere to ride on Dartmoor that you make sure the one you choose is BHS or ABRS approved. This means you will get suitable healthy, well-cared for mounts, safe equipment and insurance. The trekking centre or riding school must display a certificate declaring which association it is approved by, so you can easily check before mounting your trusty steed!

It is unlikely you will find yourself crossing Dartmoor on a Dartmoor pony, as they are only 12.2 hands in height. Most establishments use larger cobs that will carry people of all shapes and sizes, but no doubt on your travels you will come across these delightful ponies, free and wild, out on the moor.